READY-TO-EAT
STIR-FRY
Over 70 delicious one-wok meals

Caroline Hwang

Photography by Julia Stotz

hardie grant books

WOK SPATULA

WOK LID

THE ONLY TOOLS YOU NEED
FOR THIS BOOK

WOK

TONGS

STEAMER TRAY

SPIDER STRAINER

CONTENTS

STIR-FRY

The wok is one of the most versatile, efficient, yet underutilised tools in the kitchen. While mostly known for its ability to make an amazing stir-fry, it can also braise, steam, deep-fry, stew and poach, among other techniques. The smoky and slightly charred, crisp flavour you taste in a good stir-fry is called *wok hei*, which metaphorically translates to 'breath of the wok'. Cooking with a wok requires an extreme amount of high heat and although you won't get the high heat that you would get in a restaurant wok-cooked meal, you can achieve something close to it at home by using a few tips found in this book.

A well-seasoned wok creates a non-stick surface, allowing for a great sear on meats and vegetables without the worry of endless scrubbing. Due to the design of the cookware, which is lightweight and made out of thin metal, the temperature fluctuation is very different from any other cookware in your home. The shape of the wok allows the bottom of the pan to remain extra hot for searing your food,

while the sides are utilised for food to be gathered, allowing the next round of food to be cooked without steaming. This tumbling motion allows you to cook evenly and quickly.

Most of the recipes in this book are for quick and easy meals. Have your mise en place ready and you are set to go; the cooking will go by in a flash!

DESIGNING THE PERFECT STIR-FRY

Follow these easy guidelines to make your own delicious stir-fry.

1.

OIL IT UP CORRECTLY!

When cooking with a wok, you're usually cooking over high heat. It's very important to use the right oil with a high smoke point. The go-to extra virgin olive oil won't work with high heat as it makes the oil acrid. Oils are suggested in each recipe but can be swapped with other high smoke point oils, such as vegetable oil, grapeseed oil, rapeseed (canola) oil and coconut oil, among others.

2.

MAKE IT SAUCY

Most stir-fries have a base sauce to build their flavours on. There are several different sauces or condiments to vary your stir-fry, such as oyster sauce, hoisin, coconut milk and Sichuan peppercorns. You will find several recipes for sauces in the Basics chapter (see page 17) for creating a solid foundation to build your stir-fry on.

3.

PROPERLY CUT VEGETABLES ARE KEY TO A GOOD STIR-FRY

You want your veggies to be colourful and properly cooked rather than brown and mushy. Be careful about when to add quick cooking vegetables, such as (bell) peppers or spinach, or how small or large to cut your vegetables, to ensure cooking them at the same rate as your other vegetables or proteins.

4.

CHOICE OF PROTEIN

Protein doesn't have to mean poultry or red meat. Tofu and eggs make great additions to a good wok bowl, plus they create a well-balanced meal.

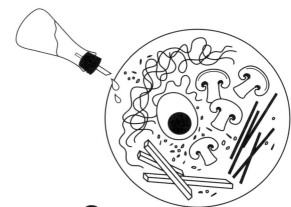

5.

PICK A STARCH, ANY STARCH

Most Asian meals are eaten with a starchy food, such as noodles or rice. The varieties are endless and it makes for a well-rounded meal, especially if your stir-fry is just vegetables. Don't be afraid to try new starches or even mix your bowl with a different grain or two.

6.

MISE EN PLACE! NO, REALLY, GET IT TOGETHER.

Make sure you have everything ready and set to go. Cut all your vegetables and mix all your sauces ready to be tossed in, on the fly. Cooking in a wok, especially over high heat, is meant to be fast and quick.

7.

BATCH COOKING

Don't overcrowd the wok! By stir-frying in batches, you will avoid overcrowding and losing too much heat. Cook a couple of ingredients at a time and remove into a bowl until all the ingredients are cooked. Then return everything to the wok and stir to combine along with any sauce.

8.

ADD AN EXTRA SOMETHING

Top your stir-fry with a crunch, such as toasted sesame seeds or extra flavour or spice, such as Quick Kimchi (see page 36). Sometimes, even a drizzle of sesame oil brings out the balance in the dish you never knew was missing.

9

WOK TIPS

Woks are very versatile and there is a wide variety available, so choosing the right wok is important. Follow these helpful hints so you can cook perfects stir-fries every time.

CHOOSING YOUR WOK

Depending on your stove, you will want a round-bottomed wok (for gas) or a flat-bottomed wok (for electric). Also, be sure to get a carbon steel rather than a non-stick or stainless steel one as you want one that spreads heat evenly and is oil-friendly. Woks with wooden handles versus two metal loops are far more versatile to work with.

SEASONING YOUR WOK

Now that you know which wok to buy, let's talk about seasoning it. When you first purchase your wok it will be covered in a grease or oil, which must be removed, then you need to season the wok prior to using it. Using hot water, soap and a scratch-free scouring pad, scrub out the oil/grease until there is none left. Dry the wok over a high heat until it begins to smoke (keep your windows open or your extractor fan on), then using tongs, wipe the inside of the wok with oil and kitchen paper. Do this once more and you have a seasoned wok.

CARING FOR YOUR WOK

To clean or wash your wok you should avoid using soap in the wok as much as possible; use the soft side of a sponge to wipe out any remaining food bits and oil. Be sure to dry the wok over low heat on the stove or using kitchen paper or a cloth.

PRE-HEATING

You also want to make sure you heat your wok over a high heat (when you flick a drop of water, it should evaporate immediately) prior to adding any oil to the wok. Most of the recipes in this book call for a high heat unless otherwise stated.

THE VERSATILITY OF THE WOK

After you have chosen and seasoned your wok you can use it for a variety of different cooking techniques, from stir-frying vegetables and meat to steaming dumplings.

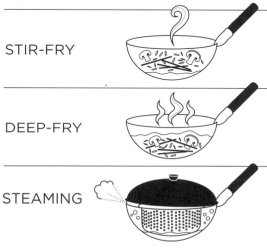

STIR-FRY

The wok lends itself well to stir-frying due to its bowl-like shape and its ability to heat up fast.

DEEP-FRY

The shape and depth of the wok allows it to hold the large amount of oil needed to deep-fry ingredients.

STEAMING

You will need an extra accessory for steaming, such as a steam pan, steam basket or a plate. Lay vegetables, meat, fish or tofu on your steam basket over 2.5–5 cm (1–2 in) water and cover with a wok lid or a baking tray.

SUBSTITUTING INGREDIENTS

- Tonkatsu sauce may be difficult to find in your local shops so use HP or steak sauce instead.
- If you can't buy gochugaru (Korean red pepper flakes), then crushed red pepper or Aleppo pepper is a great substitute.
- Gochujang is an ingredient that's very difficult to replicate, but the following recipe is probably as close as you can get.

Makes: 75 ml (2½ fl oz/⅓ cup)

1 tablespoon red miso
3 tablespoons Aleppo pepper
1 teaspoon sugar
1 tablespoon minced garlic
1 teaspoon soy sauce
1 teaspoon mirin
1 teaspoon sesame oil

recipe

Mix together all the ingredients and let sit at room temperature for 1 hour. Add water if it is too thick, but it should be the consistency of a thick paste. Refrigerate and use as needed.

NOODLES & RICE, OH MY!

There is a wide range of different types of noodles and rice available in the shops, so here are some suggestions to help you make your stir-fries interesting.

DRIED WHEAT
NOODLES

SWEET POTATO NOODLES

SOMEN

JASMINE RICE

SUSHI RICE

FRESH UDON
NOODLES

12

SHORT-GRAIN
BROWN RICE

VERMICELLI NOODLES

FRESH WHEAT NOODLES

DRIED UDON NOODLES

SOBA

FLAT RICE NOODLES

FRESH WIDE WHEAT NOODLES

BUILDING AN ASIAN PANTRY

Here is a guide to all the essential ingredients for a well-stocked pantry.

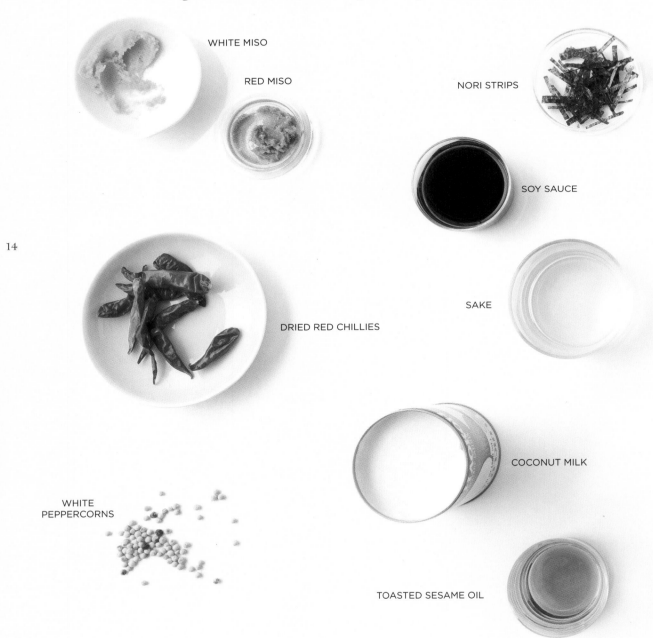

WHITE MISO

RED MISO

NORI STRIPS

SOY SAUCE

SAKE

DRIED RED CHILLIES

COCONUT MILK

WHITE
PEPPERCORNS

TOASTED SESAME OIL

14

DARK SOY SAUCE

TAMARIND PASTE

KOMBU

TOASTED SESAME SEEDS

SICHUAN PEPPERCORNS

MIRIN

FISH SAUCE

CURRY POWDER

OYSTER SAUCE

RICE VINEGAR

GOCHUGARU

BASICS

To get started on your stir-fries, you need a basic and balanced mix of sauces. Here you will find the base flavour profile to start you off, along with some tasty pickled side dishes that are quick and easy to pull together.

STIR-FRY SAUCE

Preparation: 2 minutes

makes: 190 ml (6½ fl oz/¾ cup)

100 ml (3½ fl oz/scant ½ cup) dark soy sauce
60 ml (2 fl oz/¼ cup) light soy sauce
2 tablespoons Chinese cooking wine or dry sherry
1 teaspoon ground white pepper

recipe

Combine all the ingredients in a jar or container and keep in a cool, dry place. Store for up to 2 months.

SWEETENED SESAME SOY

Preparation: 2 minutes

makes: 230 ml (7¾ fl oz/scant 1 cup)

150 ml (5 fl oz/generous ½ cup) soy sauce
2 tablespoons sesame oil
2 tablespoons finely chopped garlic
2½ tablespoons honey
1 tablespoon gochugaru
1 tablespoon toasted sesame seeds

recipe

Combine all the ingredients in a jar or bottle and keep in the refrigerator for up to 2 weeks.

NUOC CHAM BASE SAUCE

Preparation: 2 minutes

makes: 365 ml (12½ fl oz/scant 1½ cups)

120 ml (4 fl oz/½ cup) fish sauce
120 ml (4 fl oz/½ cup) rice vinegar
120 ml (4 fl oz/½ cup) lime juice
65 g (2¼ oz/generous ¼ cup) sugar
4 garlic cloves, finely chopped

recipe

Combine all the ingredients together and store in a jar or container. Keep in the refrigerator for up to 2 weeks.

JAPANESE BASE SAUCE

Preparation: 2 minutes

makes: 275 ml (9½ fl oz/generous 1 cup)

150 ml (5 fl oz/generous ½ cup) soy sauce
60 ml (2 fl oz/¼ cup) mirin
60 ml (2 fl oz/¼ cup) sake
2 tablespoons sugar

25

recipe

Combine all the ingredients together in a jar or container and store in a cool, dry place for up to a month.

COCONUT BASE SAUCE

Preparation: 2 minutes
Cooking: 2 minutes

makes: 450 ml (15½ fl oz/1¾ cups)

400 ml (14 fl oz) tin coconut milk
2 tablespoons sugar
3 tablespoons fish sauce

recipe

Combine the coconut milk and sugar in a small saucepan and warm until the sugar has dissolved. Place in a small container or jar along with the fish sauce and store in the refrigerator for up to 2 weeks.

SWEET & SPICY SAUCE

Preparation: 2 minutes

makes: 150 ml (5 fl oz/generous ½ cup)

75 g (2½ oz) gochujang (see page 11)
2 tablespoons finely chopped garlic
2 tablespoons soy sauce
2 tablespoons sugar
2 tablespoons mirin

recipe

Combine all the ingredients in a small jar and mix thoroughly until everything is combined. Store in the refrigerator for up to 2 weeks.

SICHUAN OIL

Preparation: 10 minutes + Infusion: 2 hours

makes: 250 ml (8½ fl oz/1 cup)

250 ml (8½ fl oz/1 cup) rapeseed (canola) oil
6 garlic cloves, smashed and peeled
4 cm (1½ in) knob of fresh ginger
3 whole star anise
2 cinnamon sticks
2 teaspoons whole coriander seeds
1½ tablespoons Sichuan peppercorns
2 teaspoons gochugaru
1 tablespoon soy sauce
1 teaspoon salt

recipe

Combine the oil, garlic, ginger, star anise, cinnamon and coriander seeds in a small saucepan and simmer over a low heat, letting the spices and oil infuse for 2 hours. In a small metal or heatproof bowl, combine the remaining ingredients. When the infused oil is done simmering, pour the hot oil over a sieve into the bowl of gochugaru mix. Store in an airtight jar for up to 4 weeks.

PICKLED MUSTARD GREENS

Preparation: 6 minutes + Marinade: overnight
Cooking: 2 minutes

makes: 1 litre (34 fl oz/4 cups)

1 litre (34 fl oz/4 cups) water
4 tablespoons salt
5 tablespoons sugar
1 tablespoon white distilled vinegar
½ teaspoon Sichuan peppercorns (optional)
350 g (12 oz) gai choy (Asian mustard greens)
½ onion, sliced

recipe

Combine the water with the salt, sugar, vinegar and peppercorns (if using) in a small saucepan. Bring to a simmer and take off the heat. Pour over the mustard greens and onion, place in a jar or container and let pickle overnight. Keep in the refrigerator for up to a month.

PICKLED BIRD'S-EYE CHILLIES

Preparation: 4 minutes + Marinade: 12–48 hours

makes: 180 ml (6 fl oz/¾ cup)

40 g (1½ oz) bird's-eye chillies, cut into 5 mm (¼ in) slices
60 ml (2 fl oz/¼ cup) fish sauce
120 ml (4 fl oz/½ cup) rice vinegar

recipe

Combine all the ingredients together in a jar and let the chillies pickle for 12–48 hours at room temperature. Once pickled, store in the refrigerator for up to 4 weeks.

QUICK KIMCHI

Preparation: 35–40 minutes

makes: 700 g (1 lb 9 oz)

475 g (1 lb 1 oz) Chinese cabbage (½ head), chopped into 5 cm (2 in) pieces
4 tablespoons coarse sea salt
2 tablespoons gochugaru
2 tablespoons sambal oelek (chilli-garlic sauce)
4 garlic cloves, minced
2 tablespoons fish sauce
2 teaspoons sugar
4 spring onions (scallions), sliced into 2 cm (¾ in) pieces

recipe

Salt the cabbage in a bowl and set aside for 1 hour, turning the cabbage every 30 minutes. Meanwhile, combine the remaining ingredients in a small bowl and mix together. Once the cabbage has wilted and most of its moisture has been drawn out, rinse and squeeze out any excess water. Combine the cabbage and remaining ingredients in another bowl and toss together, making sure all the cabbage is coated. Store in an airtight container for up to 2 weeks.

NOODLES & RICE

Nothing tastes better than stir-fried noodles or fried rice mixed with some delicious veggies or protein. In this chapter you will find traditional Asian recipes as well as Asian-inspired recipes using noodles and rice as an essential part of the dish.

NOODLES WITH VEGETABLES (CHINESE)

Preparation: 5 minutes
Cooking: 15 minutes

40

serves: 2

3 tablespoons oyster sauce
1 tablespoon Stir-fry Sauce (see page 18)
2 tablespoons vegetable oil
3 garlic cloves, finely chopped
200 g (7 oz) green Chinese cabbage, chopped
100 g (3½ oz) oyster mushrooms
4 spring onion (scallion) stalks, chopped into 5 cm (2 in) pieces
425 g (15 oz) cooked udon noodles (145 g/5 oz uncooked)

recipe

Combine both sauces and set aside. Heat 1 tablespoon of the oil in a wok, add the garlic and cabbage and cook for 3 minutes, or until slightly charred; set aside. Place the remaining oil in the wok along with the mushrooms and sauté, stirring until crispy and cooked through. Place the cabbage, oyster sauce mixture and remaining ingredients back in the wok. Toss and stir-fry until combined. Divide between 2 bowls and serve.

JAPCHAE WITH MUSHROOMS (KOREAN)

Preparation: 10 minutes
Cooking: 10 minutes

serves: 2

3 tablespoons Sweetened Sesame Soy (see page 20)
2 tablespoons sugar
1 tablespoon toasted sesame oil
3 tablespoons vegetable oil
75 g (2½ oz) carrots, julienned
65 g (2¼ oz) onion, sliced
45 g (1½ oz) shiitake mushrooms, sliced
75 g (2½ oz) red (bell) pepper, sliced
100 g (3½ oz) baby spinach, roughly chopped
340 g (12 oz) cooked sweet potato noodles (80 g/3 oz uncooked)

recipe

Combine the sesame soy, sugar and sesame oil together in a bowl and set aside. Heat the vegetable oil in a wok, add the carrots and onions and cook for 4–5 minutes until tender; then set aside. Add the mushrooms and pepper and cook for 3–4 minutes. Add the spinach and cook until it begins to wilt; set aside. Add the noodles and stir-fry for 1 minute. Pour the sauce mixture over the noodles along with the cooked vegetables and toss until combined. Divide between 2 bowls and serve.

STIR-FRIED KIMCHI NOODLES (KOREAN)

Preparation: 10 minutes
Cooking: 15 minutes

serves: 2

1 tablespoon vegetable oil
65 g (5¾ oz) kimchi, chopped with juices (shop-bought or see page 36)
1 tablespoon toasted sesame oil
285 g (10 oz) cooked somen noodles (100 g/3½ oz uncooked)
2 tablespoons Sweet & Spicy Sauce (see page 28)
145 g (1½ oz) romaine lettuce, shredded
nori strips, to garnish

recipe

Heat the oil in a wok over a medium-high heat and add the kimchi but set the juices aside. Cook the kimchi until wilted, about 3–4 minutes. Drizzle over ½ tablespoon of sesame oil, add the noodles, sauce and kimchi juices and stir-fry until everything is combined. Turn off the heat, drizzle over the remaining sesame oil, add the lettuce and toss. Divide between 2 bowls and garnish with nori strips.

TOFU WITH RICE (ASIAN-INSPIRED)

Preparation: 10 minutes
Cooking: 15 minutes

serves: 2

1 tablespoon Japanese Base Sauce (see page 24)
1 teaspoon rice vinegar
2 tablespoons toasted sesame oil
2 spring onions (scallions), sliced, plus extra to garnish
4 tablespoons vegetable oil
250 g (9 oz) extra firm tofu, cut into 4 cm (1½ in) pieces
2 garlic cloves, finely chopped
175 g (6 oz) green beans, cut into 4 cm (1½ in) pieces
2 eggs
330 g (11½ oz) cooked sushi rice (140 g/5 oz/⅔ cup uncooked)

recipe

Combine the sauce, vinegar, sesame oil and spring onions. Heat 3 tablespoons of vegetable oil in a wok, add the tofu and fry for 3–5 minutes on each side until golden. Set aside. Add the garlic and beans and stir-fry for 3–5 minutes until tender. Combine the tofu with the beans and stir-fry for 1 minute. Set aside. Add the remaining oil to the wok and fry the eggs for 3–5 minutes. Divide the rice and sauce mix between 2 bowls. Top with the vegetables and fried egg. Garnish with spring onions.

PAD SEE EW (THAI)

Preparation: 4 minutes
Cooking: 6 minutes

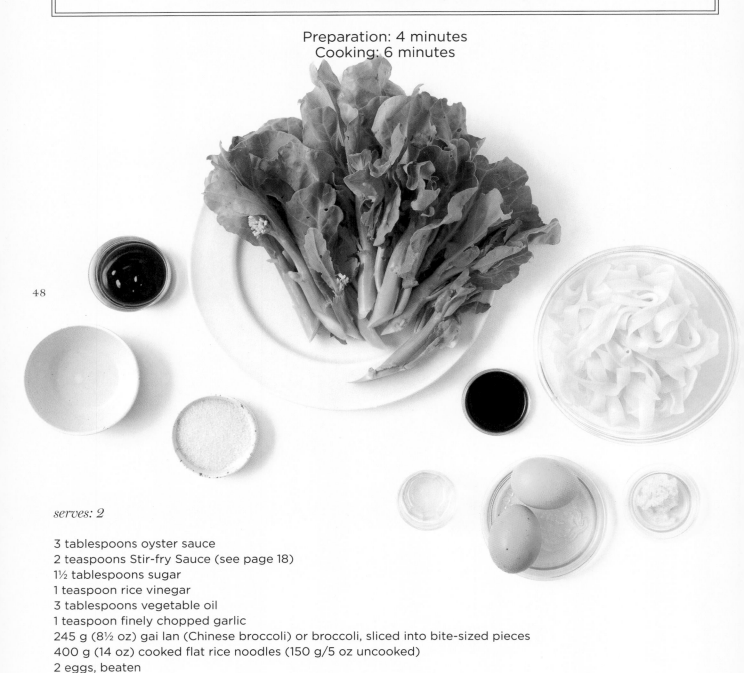

serves: 2

3 tablespoons oyster sauce
2 teaspoons Stir-fry Sauce (see page 18)
1½ tablespoons sugar
1 teaspoon rice vinegar
3 tablespoons vegetable oil
1 teaspoon finely chopped garlic
245 g (8½ oz) gai lan (Chinese broccoli) or broccoli, sliced into bite-sized pieces
400 g (14 oz) cooked flat rice noodles (150 g/5 oz uncooked)
2 eggs, beaten

recipe

Combine both the sauces, sugar and vinegar and set aside. Heat the oil in a wok, add the garlic and cook for 1 minute until fragrant. Add the gai lan and stir-fry, charring it slightly; set aside. Add the noodles and mixed sauce and stir-fry until well combined. Remove and set aside. Add the eggs and scramble until cooked through. Add the noodles and gai lan to the wok and toss. Divide between 2 bowls and serve.

PORK RICE BOWL (TAIWANESE)

Preparation: 30 minutes
Cooking: 1 hour

serves: 2

2 tablespoons vegetable oil
2 garlic cloves, thinly sliced
300 g (10½ oz) pork belly, thinly sliced
15 g (½ oz) fried shallots, crushed
1 tablespoon caster (superfine) sugar
1 tablespoon brown sugar
1 teaspoon five-spice powder
60 ml (2 fl oz/¼ cup) Stir-fry Sauce (see page 18)
35 g (1 oz) pea shoots
320 g (11¼ oz/1¾ cups) cooked jasmine rice (100 g/3½ oz/½ cup uncooked)

recipe

Heat the oil in a wok over a medium-high heat and fry the garlic for 30 seconds; set aside.
Add the pork and cook for 3–4 minutes, stirring until cooked through. Return the garlic to
the wok along with the fried shallots and stir together well. Add 70 ml (2¼ fl oz/generous
¼ cup) of water and the remaining ingredients, except the pea shoots and rice, and stir to
combine. Bring to the boil, reduce to a simmer and partially cover. Cook until the pork is
tender and the sauce is thick, about 1 hour. Divide the rice and pea shoots between
2 bowls. Top with the pork.

SCORCHED BIBIMBAP (KOREAN)

Preparation: 15 minutes
Cooking: 15 minutes

52

serves: 2

3 tablespoons vegetable oil
80 g (3 oz) carrots, julienned
80 g (3 oz) summer squash, sliced into half moons
100 g (3½ oz) spinach, roughly chopped
200 g (7 oz) cold cooked sushi rice (day old) (80 g/3 oz/⅓ cup uncooked)
2 tablespoons Sweet & Spicy Sauce (see page 28)
1 tablespoon toasted sesame oil
2 eggs

recipe

Heat the wok over a high heat, add 1 tablespoon of the vegetable oil and the carrots and cook for 2 minutes until tender. Add the remaining vegetables and cook for 3–5 minutes until tender. Season and set aside. Add 1 tablespoon of the vegetable oil to the wok with the rice and crisp the rice for 2 minutes. Lift any stuck rice from the base, stir and crisp for 2 minutes. Return the vegetables to the wok with the sauce and stir. Remove from the heat and drizzle with sesame oil. Set aside. Heat the remaining oil in the wok and fry the eggs. Divide the rice and vegetables between 2 bowls and top with the fried eggs.

LAMB PATTY RICE BOWL (ASIAN-INSPIRED)

Preparation: 12 minutes
Cooking: 5–8 minutes

serves: 2

20 g (¾ oz) coriander (cilantro) leaves
200 g (7 oz) minced lamb
1 teaspoon Sichuan peppercorns, roasted and coarsely ground
1½ teaspoons soy sauce
2 garlic cloves, finely chopped
½ teaspoon ground cumin
2 tablespoons groundnut (peanut) oil
340 g (12 oz/scant 2 cups) cooked brown rice (150 g/5 oz/¾ cup uncooked)
80 g (3 oz) baby kale

recipe

Chop half the coriander finely and set aside. Combine the lamb, peppercorns, soy sauce, garlic, cumin and chopped coriander. Divide the mixture equally into 4 patties. Heat the oil in a wok over medium-high heat and cook the patties until cooked through and golden brown, about 5–7 minutes on each side. Divide the rice and kale between 2 bowls, top with 2 patties each, then garnish with the remaining coriander.

CHICKEN PAD THAI (THAI)

Preparation: 5 minutes
Cooking: 15 minutes

serves: 2

2 tablespoons tamarind paste
4 tablespoons sugar
3 tablespoons Nuoc Cham Base Sauce (see page 22)
4 tablespoons vegetable oil
225 g (8 oz) boneless, skinless chicken breast, cut into slices
½ small onion, sliced
175 g (6 oz) broccoli, cut into small florets
2 eggs, beaten
350 g (12 oz) cooked, skinny rice noodles (150 g/5 oz uncooked)

recipe

Combine the tamarind, sugar, nuoc cham and 60 ml (2 fl oz/¼ cup) of water and set aside. Heat half oil in a wok over high heat, add the chicken and cook, turning occasionally, for 3–4 minutes. Add the onion and broccoli and cook for 5 minutes until the broccoli is tender. Set aside. Add the remaining oil and eggs and swirl in the wok. When the eggs are no longer wet, add the noodles and sauce. Stir to combine. Add the chicken and vegetables and stir-fry until well combined.

PRAWN NOODLES (VIETNAMESE)

Preparation: 14 minutes + Marinade: 1 hour
Cooking: 4 minutes

58

serves: 2

340 g (12 oz) raw prawns (shrimp) peeled, deveined with tails left on
3 tablespoons grated lemongrass
2 garlic cloves, finely chopped
3 tablespoons vegetable oil
200 g (7 oz) cooked vermicelli noodles (85 g/3 oz uncooked)
3 tablespoons mint, chopped
2 spring onion (scallion) stalks, thinly sliced on bias
1 bird's-eye red chilli, thinly sliced
120 ml (4 fl oz/½ cup) Nuoc Cham Base Sauce (see page 22), to serve

recipe

Combine the prawns, lemongrass, garlic and 2 tablespoons of oil and marinate for at least 1 hour. Heat the remaining oil in a wok over a high heat, add the prawns and stir-fry for 3–4 minutes until cooked. Divide the vermicelli noodles into 2 bowls along with the cooked prawns. Top with the remaining ingredients and serve with nuoc cham sauce.

CHICKEN YAKISOBA (JAPANESE)

Preparation: 10 minutes
Cooking: 12–15 minutes

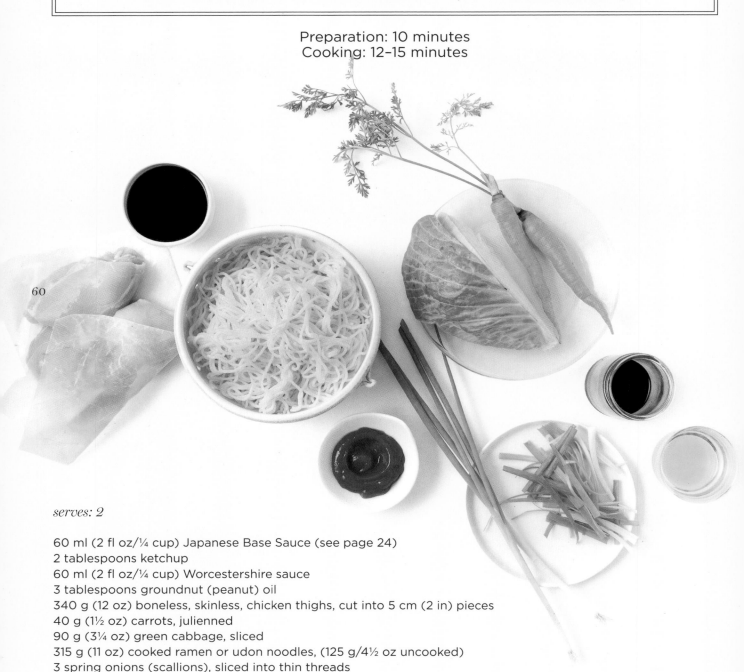

serves: 2

60 ml (2 fl oz/¼ cup) Japanese Base Sauce (see page 24)
2 tablespoons ketchup
60 ml (2 fl oz/¼ cup) Worcestershire sauce
3 tablespoons groundnut (peanut) oil
340 g (12 oz) boneless, skinless, chicken thighs, cut into 5 cm (2 in) pieces
40 g (1½ oz) carrots, julienned
90 g (3¼ oz) green cabbage, sliced
315 g (11 oz) cooked ramen or udon noodles, (125 g/4½ oz uncooked)
3 spring onions (scallions), sliced into thin threads

recipe

Combine the base sauce, ketchup and Worcestershire sauce. Heat 1 tablespoon of oil over a high heat, add the chicken and toss for 5–8 minutes until cooked through; set aside. Add the remaining oil, carrots and cabbage to the wok and stir-fry for 2 minutes. Add the noodles, combined sauces and chicken and stir-fry until evenly coated. Turn off the heat, add the spring onions and toss. Divide between 2 bowls and season with salt and white pepper.

BEEF CHOW FUN (CHINESE)

Preparation: 10 minutes + Marinade: 1 hour
Cooking: 18–20 minutes

62

serves: 2

280 g (10 oz) bavette, cut into 7 cm (2¾ oz) chunks
1 teaspoon cornflour (cornstarch)
1 teaspoon soy sauce
3 tablespoons vegetable oil
½ small onion, thinly sliced
175 g (6 oz) gai lan (Chinese broccoli) or broccoli, cut into bite-sized pieces
255 g (9 oz) cooked flat wheat noodles (170 g/6 oz uncooked)
2 tablespoons Stir-fry Sauce (see page 18)
1 teaspoon toasted sesame oil
60 g (2 oz/½ cup) beansprouts

recipe

Combine the beef, cornflour and soy sauce and marinate for 1 hour. Heat a wok over a high heat until smoking, add 1½ tablespoons of vegetable oil and the marinated beef and cook for 5 minutes until browned; set aside. Add the remaining vegetable oil to the wok with the onion and cook for 5 minutes. Add the gai lan and cook for 3–5 minutes. Toss in the noodles and stir-fry with the vegetables, sauce and sesame oil. Add the beansprouts and beef and stir-fry until everything is coated and hot. Divide between 2 bowls and serve immediately.

SPICY FAT NOODLES (SICHUAN)

Preparation: 10 minutes
Cooking: 10 minutes

64

serves: 2

2 tablespoons Stir-fry Sauce (see page 18)
2 teaspoons sugar
2 spring onions (scallions), thinly sliced
3 tablespoons groundnut (peanut) oil
2 garlic cloves, finely chopped
175 g (6 oz) pak choi (bok choy), halved or quartered
400 g (14 oz) cooked thick, fat noodles (250 g/9 oz fresh, uncooked)
3 tablespoons Sichuan Oil (see page 30)

recipe

Combine the sauce, sugar and spring onions. Heat the groundnut oil in a wok over a high heat. Add the garlic and pak choi and cook until tender, about 3–4 minutes. Add the noodles, pour in the sauce mixture and cook until the sugar is dissolved. Turn off the heat and pour Sichuan oil over the noodles and mix until thoroughly combined. Season with white pepper to taste. Divide between 2 bowls and serve.

TURMERIC PORK FRIED RICE (VIETNAMESE)

Preparation: 8 minutes
Cooking: 12 minutes

serves: 2

3 tablespoons grapeseed oil
2 shallots, sliced
4 spring onions (scallions), thinly sliced, plus extra to garnish
175 g (6 oz) minced pork
60 g (2 oz/scant ½ cup) fresh peas, shelled or frozen peas
320 g (11¼ oz/1¾ cups) cold cooked jasmine rice (preferably a day old) (100 g/3½ oz/½ cup uncooked)
2 eggs, beaten
3 tablespoons soy sauce
½ tablespoon ground turmeric

66

recipe

Heat the oil in a wok over a high heat, add the shallots and spring onions and cook for
2–3 minutes until the shallots are translucent. Add the pork and cook for 2 minutes,
breaking it apart as it gets cooked. Toss in the peas and cook until tender, about
4–5 minutes. Add the rice and stir-fry for 2–3 minutes. Add the beaten eggs and stir-fry
until well combined. Add the soy sauce and turmeric and stir for another minute. Garnish
with spring onions, divide betweeen 2 bowls and serve.

BEANSPROUT RICE (KOREAN)

Preparation: 5 minutes
Cooking: 10 minutes

68

serves: 2

2 tablespoons grapeseed oil
50 g (2 oz) chopped kimchi (shop-bought or see page 36)
200 g (7 oz/1⅓ cups) beansprouts
200 g (7 oz) cold cooked brown sushi rice (preferably a day old) (80 g/3 oz/⅓ cup uncooked)
2 tablespoons toasted sesame oil
60 ml (2 fl oz/¼ cup) Sweetened Sesame Soy (see page 20), plus extra to serve
2 spring onions (scallions), sliced
toasted sesame seeds, to garnish

recipe

Heat the grapeseed oil in a wok over high heat. Add the kimchi and cook for about
3–4 minutes. Add the beansprouts, rice and sesame oil and stir-fry for about 3 minutes.
Add the sauce and mix together until combined. Divide between 2 bowls and top with the
spring onions and toasted sesame seeds. Serve with extra sauce, if desired.

SOBA WITH TOFU (ASIAN-INSPIRED)

Preparation: 15 minutes
Cooking: 10 minutes

70

serves: 2

3 tablespoons toasted sesame oil
150 g (5 oz) asparagus, trimmed and cut into bite-sized pieces
75 g (2½ oz) frozen edamame (soybeans), shelled
185 g (6½ oz) pressed baked tofu, cut into 4 cm (1½ in) pieces
3 tablespoons soy sauce
1 tablespoon rice vinegar
1 tablespoon grated fresh ginger
315 g (11 oz) cooked soba noodles (125 g/4½ oz uncooked)
toasted sesame seeds, to garnish

recipe

Heat 1 tablespoon of the oil in a wok over a medium-high heat, add the asparagus and edamame and cook for 5 minutes until tender and slightly charred. Add the tofu, soy sauce and vinegar to the wok and stir-fry to combine. In a large bowl, combine the remaining ingredients and oil and toss to combine. Divide between 2 bowls and garnish with sesame seeds.

BEEF DONBURI (JAPANESE)

Preparation: 5 minutes
Cooking: 23–30 minutes

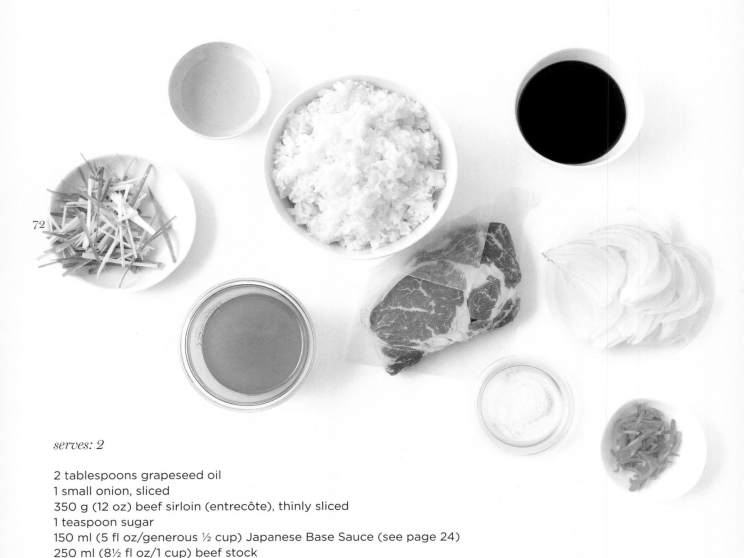

serves: 2

2 tablespoons grapeseed oil
1 small onion, sliced
350 g (12 oz) beef sirloin (entrecôte), thinly sliced
1 teaspoon sugar
150 ml (5 fl oz/generous ½ cup) Japanese Base Sauce (see page 24)
250 ml (8½ fl oz/1 cup) beef stock
450 g (1 lb) cooked sushi rice (175 g/6 oz/generous ¼ cup uncooked)
2 spring onions (scallions), thinly sliced, to garnish
pickled ginger, to garnish

recipe

Heat the oil in a wok over a low heat, add the onion and cook for 10–15 minutes, stirring frequently and letting the onions start to caramelise. Add the beef and sugar and cook until the beef starts to brown, about 3–5 minutes. Add the sauce and stock and bring to a simmer for 10 minutes, or until reduced. Divide the rice between 2 bowls and top with the beef and sauce. Top with the spring onions and pickled ginger.

RABBOKKI (KOREAN)

Preparation: 10 minutes
Cooking: 20 minutes

serves: 2

4 cm (1½ in) piece of kombu, soaked in water
60 ml (2 fl oz/¼ cup) Sweet & Spicy Sauce (see page 28)
80 g (3 oz) chopped cabbage
½ small onion, sliced
8 frozen dumplings
150 g (5 oz) dry ramen noodles
1 spring onion (scallion), sliced on bias, to garnish
sesame seeds, to garnish

recipe

Place 600 ml (20 fl oz/2⅓ cups) of water and the kombu in a wok over a high heat and bring to the boil. Remove the kombu, add the sauce and let the sauce dissolve completely. Add the remaining ingredients, except the spring onion and sesame seeds, and cook until the noodles and dumplings are cooked through and the stock has thickened. Divide between 2 bowls and top with the spring onions and sesame seeds.

DRY CURRY RICE BOWL (JAPANESE)

Preparation: 15 minutes
Cooking: 10 minutes

serves: 2

3 tablespoons curry powder or garam masala
2 tablespoons Japanese Base Sauce (see page 24)
2 tablespoons grapeseed oil
1 garlic clove, finely chopped
½ small green (bell) pepper, diced
95 g (3¼ oz) onion, diced
330 g (11½ oz) minced pork
330 g (11½ oz/1¾ cups) cooked white short-grain rice (145 g/5 oz/⅔ cup uncooked)
Quick Kimchi (see page 36), to serve (optional)

recipe

Combine the curry powder and base sauce and set aside. Heat the oil in a wok over medium-high heat, add the garlic, pepper and onion and cook for about 3 minutes. Add the pork and cook through, about 4–5 minutes. Stir in the combined sauce, add the rice and stir-fry until thoroughly combined. Divide between 2 bowls and serve with the kimchi, if desired.

OYAKODON (JAPANESE)

Preparation: 10 minutes
Cooking: 18–25 minutes

78

serves: 2

1 tablespoon vegetable oil
1 small onion, sliced
175 ml (6 fl oz/⅔ cup) chicken stock
3 tablespoons Japanese Base Sauce (see page 24)
½ teaspoon sugar
200 g (7 oz) chicken thighs and breasts, chopped into bite-sized pieces
2 eggs, beaten
330 g (11½ oz/1¾ cups) cooked white short-grain rice (145 g/5 oz/⅔ cup uncooked)
1 spring onion (scallion), thinly sliced, to garnish

recipe

Heat the wok over a medium-high heat, add the oil and onion and cook for 3–5 minutes until translucent. Add the stock, sauce and sugar and bring to a simmer. Add the chicken and cook in the stock until cooked through, about 10–15 minutes. Pour the eggs into the wok and cook until not quite fully cooked and slightly runny. Divide the rice between 2 bowls and top with the chicken mixture. Garnish with spring onions.

SPICY CUMIN LAMB NOODLES (SICHUAN)

Preparation: 15 minutes + Marinade: 1 hour
Cooking: 10 minutes

serves: 2

250 g (9 oz) lamb shoulder, thinly sliced
2 teaspoons cumin seeds, toasted, plus extra to garnish
2 garlic cloves, finely chopped
1 tablespoon Stir-fry Sauce (see page 18)
4 teaspoons Sichuan Oil (see page 30)
1 tablespoon vegetable oil
75 g (2½ oz) red onion, sliced
400 g (14 oz) cooked fresh wheat noodles (250 g/9 oz uncooked)
20 g (¾ oz) coriander (cilantro), chopped, to garnish

recipe

Combine the lamb, cumin, garlic, sauce, 100 ml (3½ fl oz/scant ½ cup) of water and half of the Sichuan oil. Marinate for at least 1 hour in the refrigerator. Heat the vegetable oil in a wok over a high heat, add the marinated lamb and red onion and stir-fry for about 5 minutes. Add the noodles and stir-fry until well combined. Take the wok off the heat and drizzle over the remaining Sichuan oil. Divide evenly between 2 bowls and garnish with the coriander.

VEGETABLES

This chapter is full of simple vegetable recipes that can be served on their own or over rice or noodles. Quickly stir-fry Oyster Mushrooms with Red Curry (see page 98) or create a delicious stew, such as the Soondubu Stew on page 124.

SICHUAN AUBERGINE WITH JASMINE RICE

Preparation: 5 minutes
Cooking: 30 minutes

serves: 2

1 teaspoon Stir-fry Sauce (see page 18)
1 tablespoon sugar
1 teaspoon arrowroot
2 tablespoons groundnut (peanut) oil
3 garlic cloves, finely chopped
1–2 teaspoons Sichuan peppercorns, coarsely ground (depending on spice level)
3 spring onions (scallions), thinly sliced
2 Asian aubergines (eggplants) (about 450 g/1 lb), cut into 3 cm (1¼ in) rounds on bias
320 g (11¼ oz/1¾ cups) cooked jasmine rice (100 g/3½ oz/½ cup uncooked)

recipe

Combine the sauce, sugar, arrowroot and 110 ml (3¾ fl oz/scant ½ cup) of water and set aside. Heat the oil in a wok over medium-high heat, add the garlic, peppercorns and 2 spring onions and stir-fry for 1 minute until fragrant. Add the aubergine and stir-fry for 5 minutes. Add the combined sauces, lower the heat and simmer for 20 minutes, stirring occasionally. Divide the rice between 2 bowls, top with the aubergine and garnish with the remaining spring onion.

PAK CHOI & TOFU (ASIAN-INSPIRED)

Preparation: 10 minutes
Cooking: 8–10 minutes

serves: 2

1 tablespoon Stir-fry Sauce (see page 18)
3 tablespoons hoisin sauce
2 teaspoons sambal oelek (chilli-garlic sauce)
2 tablespoons vegetable oil
250 g (9 oz) extra-firm tofu, cut into 2.5 cm (1 in) pieces
2 teaspoons grated fresh ginger
325 g (11½ oz) pak choi (bok choy)(or 4–6 heads), halved and quartered
fried shallots, to garnish

recipe

Combine all three sauces and set aside. Heat the wok over a high heat along with the oil. Add the tofu and stir-fry for 5–8 minutes until brown and crisp. Add the ginger and pak choi and stir occasionally until tender but still bright green, about 2 minutes. Add the sauce mixture and toss together until combined. Divide between 2 bowls, then serve garnished with crispy fried shallots.

GINGER & ASPARAGUS (ASIAN-INSPIRED)

Preparation: 5 minutes + Marinade: 2 hours
Cooking: 5 minutes

serves: 2

60 ml (2 fl oz/¼ cup) soy sauce
60 ml (2 fl oz/¼ cup) sherry vinegar
2 eggs, hard-boiled and peeled
1 teaspoon vegetable oil
4 garlic cloves, finely chopped
3 tablespoons slivered fresh ginger
350 g (12 oz) asparagus, cut into 2.5 cm (1 in) pieces
1 teaspoon toasted sesame oil
coriander (cilantro) sprigs, to garnish

recipe

Place the soy sauce and vinegar in a bowl and add the eggs. Marinate in the refrigerator for at least 2 hours. Add the oil to a wok with the garlic and ginger and heat until fragrant, about 1 minute. Add the asparagus and stir-fry until tender. Top with the sesame oil and toss until combined. Season with salt and pepper. Divide between 2 bowls, top with the soy eggs, and garnish with coriander.

CHARRED LONG GREEN BEANS (SICHUAN)

Preparation: 5 minutes
Cooking: 15 minutes

90

serves: 2

1 tablespoon Stir-fry Sauce (see page 18)
1 teaspoon sambal oelek (chilli-garlic sauce)
1 teaspoon sugar
2 tablespoons vegetable oil
200 g (7 oz) long beans or green beans, chopped into 5 cm (2 in) pieces
1 tablespoon finely chopped garlic
1 tablespoon grated fresh ginger
2 spring onions (scallions), chopped
340 g (12 oz/scant 2 cups) cooked brown rice (150 g/5 oz/¾ cup uncooked)
chilli flakes (optional)

recipe

Combine the sauces and sugar and set aside. Heat 1 tablespoon of oil in a wok over high heat, add the long beans and fry for 5 minutes until charred and the beans start to pucker. Set aside. Add the remaining oil to the wok along with the garlic, ginger and spring onions and fry for 1–2 minutes until fragrant. Return the beans to the wok and stir-fry for 3–5 minutes. Add the sauce mix and toss together. Divide the rice between 2 bowls and top with the beans and chilli flakes, if desired.

TOFU & CHIVES (JAPANESE)

Preparation: 5 minutes
Cooking: 10 minutes

serves: 2

2 tablespoons vegetable oil
35 g (1¼ oz) shiitake mushrooms, thinly sliced
100 g (3½ oz) garlic chives and chive flowers, chopped
240 g (8½ oz) medium firm tofu, crumbled
4 tablespoons Japanese Base Sauce (see page 24)
330 g (11½ oz) cooked sushi rice (145 g/5 oz/⅔ cup uncooked)
thinly sliced nori strips, to garnish (optional)

recipe

Heat the oil in a wok, add the mushrooms and cook for 5 minutes until crispy and tender.
Add the chives and sauté for about 2–3 minutes. Add the tofu and sauce and stir-fry until
everything is coated evenly. Divide the rice between 2 bowls and top with the tofu and
chive mixture. Garnish with nori strips, if desired.

PEA SHOOTS WITH GINGER (CHINESE)

Preparation: 10 minutes
Cooking: 15 minutes

serves: 2

2 tablespoons grapeseed oil
2 dried red chillies
1 tablespoon grated fresh ginger
1 tablespoon finely chopped garlic
225 g (8 oz) pea shoots, rinsed
1 teaspoon mirin
285 g (10 oz) silken tofu, crumbled into large pieces
1 tablespoon toasted sesame oil

recipe

Heat the oil and chillies in a wok over medium heat, add the ginger and garlic and heat until fragrant, about 1 minute. In four batches, add the pea shoots to the wok and cook, tossing frequently. When the stems become tender, add the mirin and silken tofu and toss once more. Drizzle over the sesame oil and season with salt and pepper. Divide between 2 bowls and serve.

MISO BROCCOLI (JAPANESE)

Preparation: 10 minutes
Cooking: 15 minutes

serves: 2

2 tablespoons Japanese Base Sauce (see page 24)
4 teaspoons miso paste
2 teaspoons rice vinegar
3 tablespoons vegetable oil
100 g (3½ oz) mixed wild mushrooms
1½ teaspoons grated fresh ginger
250 g (9 oz) tender-stem broccoli (broccolini)
340 g (12 oz) cooked sushi rice (150 g/5 oz/scant ¾ cup uncooked)

recipe

Mix the sauce and 1 teaspoon of miso together; set aside. Mix the remaining miso and the rice vinegar in a separate bowl; set aside. Heat 2 tablespoons of oil in a wok, add the mushrooms and cook until crispy and golden. Set aside. Add the remaining oil and cook the ginger and broccoli until tender, about 4 minutes. Add the miso mixture and stir-fry for 1–2 minutes. Mix the vinegar mixture and mushrooms into the rice until combined. Divide between 2 bowls, then serve topped with the broccoli.

MUSHROOMS WITH RED CURRY (THAI)

Preparation: 5 minutes
Cooking: 15 minutes

98

serves: 2

3 tablespoons coconut oil
1 small red (bell) pepper, diced
75 g (2½ oz) onion, diced
1 garlic clove, finely chopped
125 g (4 oz) oyster mushrooms
1 bunch of spring greens (about 150 g/5 oz), stemmed and chopped
1½ teaspoons red curry paste
150 ml (5 fl oz/generous ½ cup) Coconut Base Sauce (see page 26)
8 g (½ oz) Thai basil, chopped

recipe

Heat 2 tablespoons of coconut oil in a wok, add the pepper, onion and garlic and sauté for 3–4 minutes until tender; set aside. Add the mushrooms and stir-fry for 5 minutes until cooked. Add the spring greens and cook until wilted; set aside. Heat the remaining oil in the wok and add the curry paste, stirring to make sure it is cooked. Add the coconut sauce and return the vegetables to the wok. Stir to combine. Divide between 2 bowls and top with basil.

LEAFY GREENS WITH MUSHROOMS (THAI)

Preparation: 5 minutes
Cooking: 15 minutes

serves: 2

2 tablespoons groundnut (peanut) oil
2 shallots, sliced
90 g (3½ oz) honshimeji (beech) mushrooms, trimmed
2 garlic cloves, finely chopped
1 tablespoon fresh ginger, grated
1–2 bird's-eye chillies, plus extra to garnish
250 g (9 oz) mixed hearty greens, such as Swiss chard, kale, spring greens
60 ml (2 fl oz/¼ cup) Coconut Base Sauce (see page 26)

recipe

Heat 1 tablespoon of oil in a wok, add the shallots and mushrooms and cook for 3–4 minutes until the mushrooms are tender. Set aside. Add the remaining oil to the wok along with the garlic, ginger and chillies and cook for 1–2 minutes until fragrant. Add the greens and cook until wilted. Add the coconut base sauce and 3 tablespoons of water, reduce the heat to low and simmer for 10 minutes until the greens are tender. Return the mushrooms to the wok and stir to combine. Divide between 2 bowls and garnish with the chillies.

TAMARIND TOFU WITH PEPPERS (THAI)

Preparation: 10 minutes
Cooking: 15 minutes

102

serves: 2

100 ml (3½ fl oz/scant ½ cup) Coconut Base Sauce (see page 26)
1 tablespoon tamarind pulp
1 teaspoon arrowroot
3 tablespoons vegetable oil
300 g (10½ oz) extra-firm tofu, drain, pat dry and cut into triangles
2 garlic cloves, finely chopped
280 g (10 oz) sweet (bell) peppers, quartered
1 corn cob, kernels off the cob
385 g (13½ oz) steamed sticky glutinous rice (150 g/5½ oz/¾ cup uncooked)

recipe

Combine the sauce, 3 tablespoons of water, the tamarind and arrowroot and stir until dissolved. Heat 2 tablespoons of oil in a wok, add the tofu and stir-fry for 2–3 minutes each side until golden. Set aside. Add the remaining oil to the wok, add the garlic and cook for 1 minute until fragrant. Add the peppers and corn and cook until tender. Add the sauce and cook until thickened. Return the tofu and stir to combine. Divide the rice between 2 bowls and top with the tofu and peppers.

SQUASH & TOFU STIR-FRY (KOREAN)

Preparation: 5 minutes
Cooking: 15 minutes

104

serves: 2

3 tablespoons vegetable oil
½ small onion, chopped
2 garlic cloves, finely chopped
100 g (3½ oz) kimchi, chopped (shop-bought or see page 36)
280 g (10 oz) summer squash, sliced
225 g (8 oz) extra-firm tofu, cubed
4 tablespoons kimchi juice
1 tablespoon toasted sesame oil
1 tablespoon dark soy sauce
sesame seeds, to garnish

recipe

Heat 1 tablespoon oil in a wok, add the onion and cook until translucent. Add the garlic, kimchi and squash and sauté for 3–4 minutes. Set aside. Add the remaining oil to the wok and stir-fry the tofu for 5 minutes until crisp and browned. Return the cooked kimchi and squash mixture to the wok along with the remaining ingredients, except the sesame seeds. Toss and stir-fry until thoroughly combined and coated. Divide between 2 bowls and garnish with sesame seeds.

BROCCOLI WITH MUSHROOMS (CHINESE)

Preparation: 5 minutes
Cooking: 20 minutes

serves: 2

2 tablespoons vegetable oil
250 g (9 oz) mixed mushrooms
1 tablespoon grated fresh ginger
3 garlic cloves, finely chopped
300 g (10½ oz) broccoli, cut into small florets
1 tablespoon Stir-fry Sauce (see page 18)
2 tablespoons oyster sauce
2 spring onions (scallions), finely slivered, to garnish

recipe

Heat 1 tablespoon of oil in a wok, add the mushrooms and cook for 5 minutes until golden; set aside. Add the remaining oil to the wok, add ginger and the garlic and cook for 1–2 minutes until fragrant. Add the broccoli and stir-fry until tender. Add the sauces and mushrooms to the wok and stir-fry to combine. Divide between 2 bowls and top with the spring onions.

SUGAR SNAP PEAS WITH EGGS (CHINESE)

Preparation: 20 minutes
Cooking: 5 minutes

serves: 2

2 tablespoons vegetable oil
2 shallots, thinly sliced
8 cm (3¼ in) knob of fresh ginger, cut into thin strips
280 g (10 oz) sugar snap peas, halved
1 tablespoon toasted sesame oil
handful of pea shoots
2 eggs, poached
salt and freshly ground pepper

recipe

Heat the vegetable oil in a hot wok over high heat, add the shallots and ginger and fry until fragrant, about 30 seconds. Add the sugar snap peas and sesame oil and toss for 3 minutes until tender. Divide the pea shoots and sugar snap peas between 2 bowls. Top with a poached egg and season with salt and pepper to taste.

MISO BEANS & POTATOES (JAPANESE)

Preparation: 10 minutes
Cooking: 16–20 minutes

110

serves: 2

60 g (2 oz) white miso paste
60 ml (2 fl oz/¼ cup) mirin
60 ml (2 fl oz/¼ cup) honey
1 tablespoon grated fresh ginger
1 tablespoon toasted sesame oil
400 g (14 oz) small new potatoes, halved
2 tablespoons vegetable oil
175 g (6 oz) green beans, cut into bite-sized pieces
toasted sesame seeds, to garnish

recipe

Combine the miso, mirin, honey, ginger and sesame oil and set aside. Place the potatoes in a wok and cover with 120 ml (4 fl oz/½ cup) of water. Heat over a medium heat, bring to a simmer, cover and cook for 8–10 minutes, or until tender. Add the vegetable oil to the wok and bring the heat to high. Add the beans and stir-fry for 8–10 minutes until cooked through and the potatoes are crisp. Add the miso mixture and coat thoroughly. Divide between 2 bowls and garnish with sesame seeds.

POTATO CROQUETTES (JAPANESE)

Preparation: 5 minutes + Refrigeration: 1 hour
Cooking: 18–25 minutes

serves: 2

700 g (1 lb 9 oz) Yukon Gold or Charlotte potatoes, peeled and chopped into 3 cm (1¼ in) pieces
350 ml (12 fl oz/generous 1⅓ cups) vegetable oil, plus 1 tablespoon
2 spring onions (scallions), thinly sliced
50 g (2 oz/⅓ cup) plain (all-purpose) flour
2 eggs, beaten
75 g (2½ oz) panko breadcrumbs
150 g (5 oz) green cabbage, thinly shaved
3 tablespoons rice vinegar
Tonkatsu sauce (or HP or steak sauce), for topping

recipe

Place the potatoes in a wok, cover with water and bring to the boil. Cover with a lid and simmer for 15–20 minutes until cooked. Drain the potatoes and mash with 1 tablespoon of oil. Add the spring onions, season and mix well. When cool enough to handle, form the mixture into 8–10 oval patties and chill for 1 hour. Coat the patties with flour, eggs, then the panko. Heat the oil in the wok to 180°C (350°F) and deep-fry the patties for 3–5 minutes until golden. Mix the cabbage with the vinegar and season. Serve the patties with the Tonkatsu sauce and cabbage.

GARLIC CHIVE EGGS (JAPANESE)

Preparation: 5 minutes
Cooking: 10 minutes

serves: 2

4 eggs, whisked in a bowl
1 teaspoon Japanese Base Sauce (see page 24)
2 tablespoons safflower oil or any vegetable oil
60 g (2 oz) garlic chives, chopped
salt and freshly ground pepper
330 g (11½ oz) cooked sushi brown rice (145 g/5 oz/⅔ cup uncooked)

recipe

Combine the eggs and sauce and set aside. Heat 1 tablespoon of oil in a wok over high heat, add the garlic chives and stir-fry until tender, about 2 minutes. Place the cooked chives in the egg mixture. Heat the remaining oil in the wok over a high heat until smoking, add the egg and chive mixture to the wok and gently fold the egg mixture from outside in until cooked through. Season to taste. Divide the rice and eggs between 2 bowls.

TOFU & GARLIC PEPPER SAUCE (CHINESE)

Preparation: 15 minutes
Cooking: 10 minutes

116

serves: 2

2 tablespoons Stir-fry Sauce (see page 18)
2 tablespoons sugar
400 g (14 oz) firm tofu, sliced into 4 cm (1½ in) cubes
1 teaspoon arrowroot
60 ml (2 fl oz/¼ cup) vegetable oil
6 garlic cloves, finely chopped
2 tablespoons grated fresh ginger
4 shallots, thinly sliced
2 jalapeño chillies, thinly sliced
3 tablespoons black peppercorns, coarsely ground

recipe

Combine the sauce, sugar and 125 ml (4 fl oz/½ cup) of water. Dust the tofu with the arrowroot, shaking off the excess. Heat half the oil in a wok, add the tofu and fry until golden on all sides, about 3–4 minutes. Set aside. Add the remaining oil to the wok and lower the heat to medium-high. Add the garlic, ginger, shallots and chillies and cook for 1–2 minutes until fragrant and the shallots are translucent. Add the sauce with the tofu and stir-fry until combined. Toss in the peppercorns and cook for 1 minute. Divide between 2 bowls and serve immediately.

QUICK SAUTÉED MUSHROOMS (KOREAN)

Preparation: 10 minutes
Cooking: 15 minutes

118

serves: 2

2 tablespoons vegetable oil
1 small red onion, sliced
300 g (10½ oz) mixed mushrooms
2 garlic cloves, finely chopped
1 teaspoon grated fresh ginger
165 g (5¾ oz) kimchi, chopped with juices (shop-bought or see page 36)
1 tablespoon soy sauce
330 g (11½ oz/1¾ cups) cooked cold brown rice (140 g/5 oz/generous ⅔ cup uncooked)
1 tablespoon toasted sesame oil
nori strips, to garnish

recipe

Heat half the vegetable oil in a wok, add the onion and mushrooms and cook until the mushrooms are golden brown, about 5 minutes. Set aside. Add the remaining vegetable oil, garlic and ginger to the wok and cook for 1–2 minutes until fragrant. Add the kimchi with its juices and soy sauce and cook for about 2–3 minutes. Add the rice and mushrooms to the wok and stir-fry for 2 minutes. Remove from the heat and drizzle with sesame oil. Divide between 2 bowls and garnish with nori strips.

SAUTÉED SESAME SPINACH (KOREAN)

Preparation: 10 minutes
Cooking: 15 minutes

120

serves: 2

225 g (8 oz) spinach, trimmed and cleaned
225 g (8 oz) beansprouts
1 tablespoon grapeseed oil
2 garlic cloves, finely chopped
3 teaspoons soy sauce
¼ teaspoon sugar
330 g (11½ oz) cooked sushi rice (140 g/5 oz/⅔ cup uncooked)
3 teaspoons toasted sesame oil
sesame seeds, to garnish
salt and freshly ground pepper

recipe

Heat the wok over a medium heat, add the spinach, beansprouts and 60 ml (2 fl oz/¼ cup) of water and blanch the spinach and beansprouts. Remove and squeeze out excess water. Heat the grapeseed oil in the wok over a low heat and add the garlic. Add the vegetables to the wok along with 2 teaspoons of soy sauce and the sugar. Stir-fry until combined. Combine the rice, sesame oil and remaining soy sauce, divide between 2 bowls and top with the spinach and beansprout mixture. Garnish with sesame seeds and season.

STIR-FRIED TOFU & CHOY SUM (CHINESE)

Preparation: 10 minutes
Cooking: 15 minutes

122

serves: 2

2 teaspoons Stir-fry Sauce (see page 18)
1 tablespoon oyster sauce
1 teaspoon toasted sesame oil
2 tablespoons rice vinegar
2 tablespoons groundnut (peanut) oil
350 g (12 oz) extra-firm tofu, drain, pat dry and cut into 4 cm (1½ in) pieces
4 garlic cloves, finely chopped
150 g (5 oz) choy sum or pak choi (bok choy), halved or quartered if too large
2 spring onions (scallions), thinly sliced, to garnish

recipe

Combine the sauces, sesame oil and vinegar and set aside. Heat the oil in a wok over medium-high heat, add the tofu and stir-fry until golden, about 3–4 minutes. Add the garlic and cook until fragrant, about 1 minute. Add the choy sum and stir-fry for another 2 minutes. Add the sauce mixture and toss to combine. Divide between 2 bowls and top with the spring onions.

SOONDUBU STEW (KOREAN)

Preparation: 15 minutes
Cooking: 10 minutes

serves: 2

65 g (2¼ oz) shiitake mushrooms, stemmed and sliced
1 tablespoon toasted sesame oil
2 garlic cloves, finely chopped
150 g (5 oz) kimchi (shop-bought or see page 36)
1 tablespoon gochugaru or less depending on spice level
1 teaspoon fish sauce
325 g (11½ oz) silken tofu, cut into cubes
40 g (1½ oz) enoki mushrooms
1 spring onion, sliced on bias

recipe

Bring the shiitake mushrooms and 420 ml (14½ fl oz/1⅔ cups) of water to the boil in a wok over medium-high heat. Cover and simmer for 15 minutes. Leaving the mushrooms in the wok, pour the broth out and set aside. Add the oil and garlic to the mushrooms and raise the heat to high. Stir-fry for 1 minute. Add the kimchi and gochugaru and stir for 5 minutes. Add the fish sauce, tofu and broth to the wok and simmer for 15 minutes. Serve topped with enoki mushrooms and spring onion.

SPICY AUBERGINE (THAI)

Preparation: 5 minutes + Draining: 30 minutes
Cooking: 5 minutes

126

serves: 2

440 g (15½ oz) Asian aubergines (eggplants), cut into 5 cm (2 in) chunks
3 tablespoons sea salt
320 g (11¼ oz/1¾ cups) cooked jasmine rice (100 g/3½ oz/½ cup uncooked)
1 tablespoon red curry paste
3 tablespoons Coconut Base Sauce (see page 26)
2 tablespoons coconut oil
2 garlic cloves, finely chopped
1 teaspoon finely chopped fresh ginger
coriander (cilantro), to garnish

recipe

Sprinkle salt over the aubergine and leave on a kitchen-paper-lined baking tray for 30 minutes. Rinse and pat dry. Combine the curry paste, sauce and 60 ml (2 fl oz/ ¼ cup) of water and set aside. Heat the oil in a wok over medium heat, add the garlic and ginger and stir-fry for 1 minute. Add the aubergine and sear on all sides. Add the coconut base sauce mixture and cover for 3–5 minutes, or until cooked, stirring frequently. Serve garnished with the coriander.

STIR-FRIED VEGETABLES (THAI)

Preparation: 10 minutes
Cooking: 15 minutes

128

serves: 2

2 tablespoons vegetable oil
2 dried red chillies or 2 teaspoons crushed red chilli
2 garlic cloves, finely chopped
150 g (5 oz) broccoli, cut into small florets
150 g (5 oz) cauliflower, cut into small florets
1 small red (bell) pepper, chopped
160 ml (5¼ fl oz/scant ⅔ cup) Coconut Base Sauce (see page 26)
8 g (½ oz) Thai basil, chopped
45 g (1½ oz) roasted cashews, roughly chopped
salt and freshly ground pepper, if needed

recipe

Heat the oil in a wok, add the dried chillies and garlic and cook until fragrant, about
1 minute. Add the broccoli and cauliflower, season with salt and pepper and stir-fry for
4–5 minutes. Add the red pepper and cook until the vegetables are tender but still firm.
Add the sauce and stir to combine. Divide between 2 bowls and top with the basil and
roasted cashews. Season, if needed.

MEAT & POULTRY

The versatility of the wok allows you to cook meat and poultry by stir-frying, braising or frying. Whatever method you decide, this one wok cooking will make it a delicious one.

BISTEK TAGALOG (FILIPINO)

Preparation: 10 minutes + Marinade: overnight
Cooking: 15 minutes

132

serves: 2

480 g (1 lb 1 oz) beef sirloin, cubed
4 tablespoons soy sauce
3 garlic cloves, finely chopped
3 tablespoons key lime or lime juice
1 tablespoon white distilled vinegar
2 tablespoons vegetable oil
1 large onion, sliced into rings
320 g (11¼ oz/1¾ cups) cooked jasmine rice (100 g/3½ oz/½ cup uncooked)

recipe

Combine the beef, soy sauce, garlic, lime juice and vinegar and marinate, covered, in the refrigerator overnight. Heat the oil in a wok over a medium-high heat, add the onion and cook until translucent. Raise the heat to high, add the marinated beef and juices and stir-fry until medium rare. Season. Divide the rice between 2 bowls and top with the beef and onions.

BRAISED BEEF SHORT RIBS (CHINESE)

Preparation: 5 minutes + Marinade: 3 hours or overnight
Cooking: 35–50 minutes

134

serves: 2

800 g (1 lb 12 oz) short ribs, bone-in
1 tablespoon five-spice powder
60 ml (2 fl oz/¼ cup) hoisin sauce
2 tablespoons dry sherry or Shoaxing wine
1 tablespoon soy sauce
2 tablespoons honey
½ teaspoon ground white pepper
½ teaspoon garlic powder
2 tablespoons groundnut (peanut) oil

recipe

Combine all the ingredients, except for the oil, then marinate in the refrigerator for at least 3 hours, or overnight. Heat the oil in a wok, add the ribs and brown for 2 minutes on each side. Lower the heat to medium-low, add the remaining marinade and 200 ml (7 fl oz/generous ¾ cup) of water, cover and braise for 30–45 minutes until the beef is tender. Divide between 2 bowls and serve.

FIVE-SPICE PORK (CHINESE)

Preparation: 10 minutes + Marinade: 30 minutes
Cooking: 6 minutes

136

serves: 2

450 g (1 lb) pork loin, cut into cubes
2 tablespoons brown sugar
1 tablespoon five-spice powder
salt and freshly ground pepper
2 tablespoons groundnut (peanut) oil
6–8 butter lettuce leaves
2 spring onions (scallions), thinly sliced
1 Lebanese or small cucumber, sliced
1 Asian pear, julienned
3 tablespoons hoisin sauce, for dipping

recipe

Combine the pork, sugar, five-spice and salt and pepper and marinate in the refrigerator for 30 minutes. Heat the oil in a wok over a high heat, add the marinated pork and cook until tender, about 5–6 minutes. Assemble the lettuce wraps by filling with pork and topping with the spring onions, cucumber and pear. Use the hoisin sauce for dipping.

SHAKEN BEEF (VIETNAMESE)

Preparation: 5 minutes + Marinade: 1 hour
Cooking: 10 minutes

serves: 2

1 tablespoon oyster sauce
2 teaspoons Stir-fry Sauce (see page 18)
2 teaspoons fish sauce
5 garlic cloves, finely chopped
2 tablespoons sugar
425 g (15 oz) beef fillet (filet mignon), cut into 2.5 cm (1 in) cubes
2 tablespoons rapeseed (canola) oil
½ small red onion, thickly sliced
60 g (2 oz) watercress

recipe

Combine all the sauces, garlic and sugar. Add the beef and marinate in the refrigerator for 1 hour. Heat 1 tablespoon of oil in a wok over a high heat, add the onion and cook until translucent. Set aside. Heat the remaining oil and add the beef to the wok in batches and spread out in one layer. Shake the wok, searing the beef on all sides. Return the onions to the wok and cook together for 1 minute. Divide the watercress between 2 bowls and top with the beef.

BRAISED PORK BELLY (VIETNAMESE)

Preparation: 10 minutes
Cooking: 1 hour

serves: 2

225 ml (7¾ fl oz/scant 1 cup) coconut water
2 tablespoons fish sauce
2 tablespoons soy sauce
4 garlic cloves, finely chopped
450 g (1 lb) pork belly, cut into 4 cm (1½ in) pieces
salt and freshly ground pepper
170 g (6 oz/¾ cup) sugar
2 hard-boiled eggs, peeled
Pickled Mustard Greens (see page 32), to serve

recipe

Combine the coconut water, sauces and garlic. Season the pork with salt and pepper. Add the sugar to a wok over a medium-high heat. Let the sugar melt and caramelise, about 3–5 minutes. Add the pork and stir to combine. Add the coconut water mixture to the wok and bring to a simmer. Add the eggs and simmer, covered, for 1 hour. Divide between 2 bowls and serve with the pickled mustard greens.

DRY-FRIED LONG BEANS (SICHUAN)

Preparation: 5 minutes
Cooking: 20 minutes

serves: 2

100 g (3½ oz) long beans or green beans, chopped into bite-sized pieces
2 tablespoons vegetable oil
150 g (5½ oz) minced (ground) pork
2 garlic cloves, smashed and coarsely chopped
2 teaspoons chopped fresh ginger
2 teaspoons Sichuan peppercorns, toasted and coarsely ground
1 tablespoon Stir-fry Sauce (see page 18)
1 teaspoon sugar
320 g (11¼ oz/1¾ cups) cooked jasmine rice (100 g/3½ oz/½ cup uncooked)

recipe

Heat the wok over a high heat until it starts to smoke, add the beans and dry-fry for
1 minute. Reduce the heat to medium and cook until charred and tender. Set aside. Heat
the oil in the wok over a medium-high heat, add the pork and cook for 3–5 minutes until
browned. Add the garlic, ginger and peppercorns and cook for 1–2 minutes until fragrant.
Return the beans to the wok with the sauce and sugar and stir-fry until heated through.
Divide the rice between 2 bowls and top with the pork and beans.

PAD GRA PROW (THAI)

Preparation: 5 minutes
Cooking: 15 minutes

144

serves: 2

2 tablespoons vegetable oil
3 garlic cloves, finely chopped
½ shallot, finely chopped
285 g (10 oz) minced (ground) beef
115 g (4 oz) green beans, chopped into 3 cm (1¼ in) pieces
50 g (2 oz) holy basil or Thai basil, chopped, plus extra to garnish
1 tablespoon Stir-fry Sauce (see page 18)
1 tablespoon fish sauce

recipe

Heat the oil in a wok, add the garlic and shallots and cook for 1 minute. Add the beef and stir-fry for 3–5 minutes until cooked through. Set aside. Add the green beans and basil and stir-fry for 4–5 minutes until the beans are tender. Return the beef to the wok with the sauces and stir until coated all over. Divide between 2 bowls and garnish with some extra basil.

KUNG PAO CHICKEN (CHINESE)

Preparation: 10 minutes + Marinade: 1 hour
Cooking: 10 minutes

serves: 2

450 g (1 lb) skinless, boneless chicken breast, sliced
1 tablespoon arrowroot
1 tablespoon Stir-fry Sauce (see page 18)
¼ teaspoon white pepper
3 tablespoons vegetable oil
3 dried red chillies
1 teaspoon finely chopped fresh ginger
2 garlic cloves, finely chopped
75 g (2½ oz) green (bell) pepper, sliced
60 g (2 oz/generous ⅓ cup) roasted cashews, roughly chopped

recipe

Coat the chicken with the arrowroot, add the sauce, 2 tablespoons of water and the white pepper and marinate in the refrigerator for at least 1 hour. Heat half the oil in a wok over a high heat, add the chillies and toast for 1 minute. Add the ginger, garlic and green pepper and cook for 1–2 minutes until tender. Set aside. Heat the remaining oil and stir-fry the chicken for 5 minutes until cooked through. Return the green pepper mixture and stir-fry for a minute. Divide between 2 bowls and serve topped with cashews.

PRIK KING (THAI)

Preparation: 10 minutes
Cooking: 15 minutes

serves: 2

3 tablespoons grapeseed oil
4 garlic cloves, finely chopped
2 teaspoons red curry paste
450 g (1 lb) boneless chicken breast, thinly sliced
1 teaspoon fish sauce
½ teaspoon sugar
225 g (8 oz) long beans or green beans, cut into 4 cm (1½ in) pieces
3–4 kaffir lime leaves, thinly sliced
Pickled Bird's-eye Chillies (see page 34) (optional)

recipe

Heat the oil over a medium heat, add the garlic and cook for 1 minute until fragrant. Add the curry paste and fry for 30 seconds. Raise the heat to high, add the chicken and stir-fry for 5 minutes until combined. Add the fish sauce and sugar, stir and cook until the chicken is cooked through. Add the beans and lime leaves and cook for 2–3 minutes until the beans are tender. Divide between 2 bowls and serve with pickled chillies, if desired.

LEMONGRASS CHICKEN (VIETNAMESE)

Preparation: 10 minutes
Cooking: 15 minutes

150

serves: 2

3 tablespoons vegetable oil
450 g (1 lb) boneless, skinless chicken breast, cut into 2.5 cm (1 in) strips
300 g (10½ oz) broccoli, cut into small florets
50 g (2 oz) finely sliced lemongrass
2 garlic cloves, finely chopped
1 tablespoon coriander seeds, toasted and coarsely ground
1 jalapeño chilli, sliced into rings
2 tablespoons Nuoc Cham Base sauce (see page 22)
10 g (½ oz) coriander (cilantro) sprigs, to garnish

recipe

Heat the oil in a wok over high heat, add the chicken and cook for 5–8 minutes until lightly browned on all sides. Lower the heat to medium-high, add the broccoli and cook for about 2 minutes. Add the remaining ingredients, except the nuoc cham and coriander, and stir-fry for 5 minutes, deglazing with water, if necessary. Add the nuoc cham and cook, stirring, for 1 minute. Divide between 2 bowls and garnish with the coriander.

KARAAGE & MUSTARD GREENS (JAPANESE)

Preparation: 15 minutes + Marinade: 1 hour or overnight
Cooking: 15 minutes

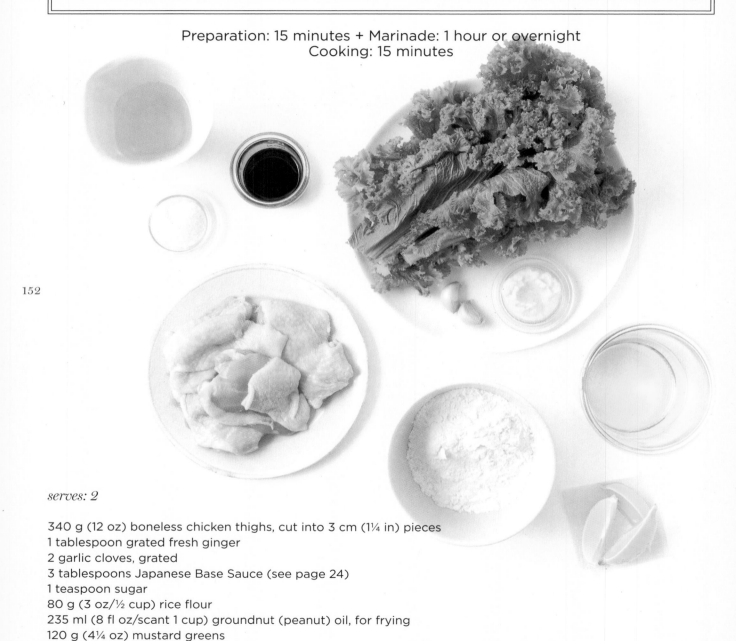

152

serves: 2

340 g (12 oz) boneless chicken thighs, cut into 3 cm (1¼ in) pieces
1 tablespoon grated fresh ginger
2 garlic cloves, grated
3 tablespoons Japanese Base Sauce (see page 24)
1 teaspoon sugar
80 g (3 oz/½ cup) rice flour
235 ml (8 fl oz/scant 1 cup) groundnut (peanut) oil, for frying
120 g (4¼ oz) mustard greens
1 tablespoon seasoned rice vinegar
lemon wedges, to garnish

recipe

Place the chicken, ginger, garlic, sauce and sugar in a small bowl and marinate in the refrigerator for at least 1 hour, or overnight. Dredge the chicken in flour while the oil is heating in a wok over medium heat until it reaches 180°C (350°F). Fry four chicken pieces at a time for 5–10 minutes or until cooked through. Place the cooked chicken on a wire rack set over a baking tray. Meanwhile, toss the mustard greens with the vinegar. Divide between 2 plates and garnish with the lemon wedges.

PORK & NOODLE STIR-FRY (SHANGHAI)

Preparation: 15 minutes
Cooking: 15 minutes

154

serves: 2

5 tablespoons groundnut (peanut) oil
2 bunches of spring onions (scallions), cut into 5 cm (2 in) pieces
1 tablespoon Stir-fry Sauce (see page 18)
2 teaspoons sugar
325 g (11½ oz) pork tenderloin, chopped into 3 cm (1¼ in) pieces
400 g (14 oz) cooked fresh white noodles (250 g/9 oz uncooked fresh)
2 teaspoons toasted sesame oil
micro-coriander (cilantro), to garnish

recipe

Heat 1 tablespoon of oil in a wok over a medium heat, add the spring onions and fry for 2 minutes. Remove from the wok. Add the sauce and sugar and bring to a simmer. Simmer for 5 minutes until slightly thickened, then set aside in a separate bowl. Add the remaining oil to the wok and cook the pork for 5 minutes until tender. Add the noodles and toss to combine. Remove from the heat and toss the fried spring onions with the thickened sauce and sesame oil. Divide between 2 bowls and garnish with the micro-coriander.

SPICY CHICKEN STIR-FRY (KOREAN)

Preparation: 10 minutes + Refrigeration: 1 hour minimum
Cooking: 20 minutes

156

serves: 2

400 g (14 oz) skinless, boneless chicken thighs, cut into 5 cm (2 in) pieces
100 ml (3½ fl oz/scant ½ cup) Sweet & Spicy Sauce (see page 28)
1 teaspoon grated fresh ginger
125 g (4 oz) sweet potatoes, cut into cubes
2 tablespoons vegetable oil
150 g (5 oz) cabbage, chopped
2 spring onions (scallions), sliced into 5 cm (2 in) pieces
nori strips, to garnish

recipe

Combine the chicken, sauce and ginger and chill for at least 1 hour. Add the sweet potatoes and 80 ml (2½ fl oz/⅓ cup) of water to a wok, cover and cook for 5 minutes until tender. Pour out the water from the wok, add the oil over a medium heat and stir-fry until the sweet potato crispy and brown. Set aside. Add the cabbage and chicken to the wok and stir-fry until the chicken is cooked, about 5–8 minutes. Add the spring onions and cook for 1 minute. Toss in the potatoes and stir to combine. Divide between 2 bowls and garnish with nori.

CHICKEN ADOBO (FILIPINO)

Preparation: 15 minutes + Marinade: 8 hours
Cooking: 30–45 minutes

158

serves: 2

2 chicken drumsticks and 2 chicken thighs, bone in and skin on (about 700 g/1 lb 9 oz)
2 tablespoons soy sauce
5 garlic cloves, thinly sliced
175 ml (6 fl oz/⅔ cup) palm vinegar (apple cider or white vinegar)
225 ml (8 fl oz/scant 1 cup) whole tinned tomatoes with liquid, crushed with hands
1 bay leaf
2 teaspoons freshly ground black pepper
3 tablespoons olive oil
½ onion, thinly sliced
salt and fresh ground black pepper, if needed

recipe

Combine all the ingredients, except the oil and onion, and marinate in the refrigerator overnight. When ready to cook, place the marinated mixture with its sauce, the oil and onion in a wok over medium heat. Cover and braise for 30–45 minutes, or cooked through and the liquid has reduced. Divide between 2 bowls and season with salt and pepper, if needed.

PEKING DUCK (CHINESE)

Preparation: 5 minutes + Marinade: 1 hour or overnight
Cooking: 5–8 minutes

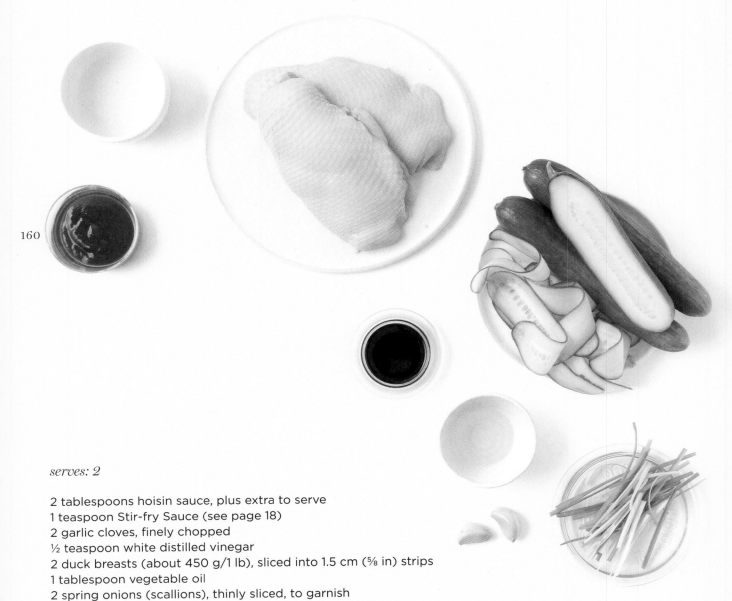

serves: 2

2 tablespoons hoisin sauce, plus extra to serve
1 teaspoon Stir-fry Sauce (see page 18)
2 garlic cloves, finely chopped
½ teaspoon white distilled vinegar
2 duck breasts (about 450 g/1 lb), sliced into 1.5 cm (⅝ in) strips
1 tablespoon vegetable oil
2 spring onions (scallions), thinly sliced, to garnish
2 cucumbers (about 150 g/5 oz), sliced thinly into ribbons

recipe

Combine both sauces, the garlic and vinegar and set aside. Score the duck skin and add to the hoisin sauce mixture. Marinate in the refrigerator for 1 hour, or overnight. Heat the oil in a wok, add the duck and sear to medium rare, about 5–8 minutes. Divide between 2 bowls. Top with the spring onions and cucumbers.

THAI-STYLE FRIED CHICKEN STRIPS (THAI)

Preparation: 5 minutes + Marinade: overnight
Cooking: 10–20 minutes

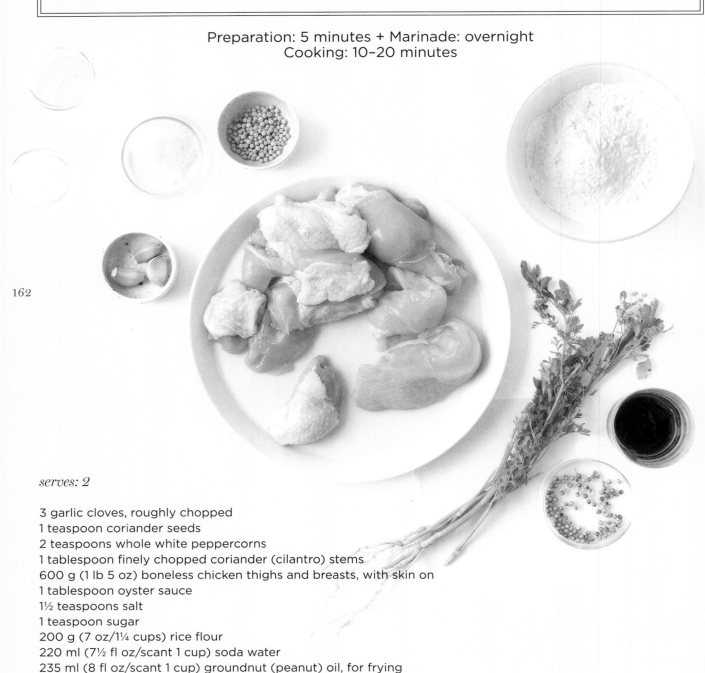

serves: 2

3 garlic cloves, roughly chopped
1 teaspoon coriander seeds
2 teaspoons whole white peppercorns
1 tablespoon finely chopped coriander (cilantro) stems
600 g (1 lb 5 oz) boneless chicken thighs and breasts, with skin on
1 tablespoon oyster sauce
1½ teaspoons salt
1 teaspoon sugar
200 g (7 oz/1¼ cups) rice flour
220 ml (7½ fl oz/scant 1 cup) soda water
235 ml (8 fl oz/scant 1 cup) groundnut (peanut) oil, for frying

recipe

Grind the garlic, coriander seeds, peppercorns and coriander stems in a mortar and pestle or food processor to a paste. Add the paste to the chicken with the oyster sauce, 1 teaspoon of salt and the sugar. Marinate in the refrigerator overnight. Make a batter by whisking 75 g (2½ oz/½ cup) of the rice flour, the soda water and remaining salt together. Dip the chicken into the batter, then coat in the remaining flour, shaking off any excess. Place on a baking tray and dry. Heat the oil to 180°C (350°F) and fry the chicken for 10–15 minutes. Drain on kitchen paper and serve.

SEAFOOD

The most popular seafood stir-fries are usually made with prawns but steaming a whole fish and searing scallops can easily be done in a wok as well. The endless versatility will surprise you.

PRAWN & SUGAR SNAP PEAS (THAI)

Preparation: 15 minutes
Cooking: 15 minutes

serves: 2

2 tablespoons coconut oil
½ shallot, finely chopped
1 tablespoon thinly sliced fresh ginger
330 g (11½ oz) raw prawns, peeled and deveined, with tails on
125 g (4 oz) sugar snap peas, halved
150 ml (5 fl oz/generous ½ cup) Coconut Base Sauce (see page 26)
1 tablespoon fish sauce
3 tablespoons fresh turmeric, grated, or 1 tablespoon ground
coriander (cilantro), to garnish

recipe

Heat 1 tablespoon of oil in a wok, add the shallots and ginger and cook for 2 minutes until fragrant. Add the prawns and stir-fry for 3–5 minutes until cooked through. Set aside. Add the remaining oil to the wok and the sugar snap peas and cook for 2 minutes. Add the remaining ingredients and the prawns and stir-fry for 2 minutes. Divide between 2 bowls and garnish with coriander.

WOK-FRIED WHOLE FISH (THAI)

Preparation: 15 minutes
Cooking: 15 minutes

168

serves: 2

125 g (4 oz) green papaya, shredded
125 g (4 oz) cherry tomatoes, halved
80 ml (2½ fl oz/⅓ cup) Nuoc Cham Base Sauce (see page 22)
175 ml (6 fl oz/⅔ cup) rapeseed (canola) oil
400 g (14 oz) whole snapper or sea bass, 3 slits cut into each side
50 g (2 oz) potato flour
2 teaspoons thinly sliced fresh ginger
2 red bird's-eye chillies, thinly sliced diagonally
15 g (½ oz) coriander (cilantro) leaves, to garnish

recipe

Combine the papaya, cherry tomatoes and half the sauce. Heat the oil in a wok over medium-high heat until it reaches 180°C (350°F). Coat the snapper with potato flour and season. Fry for 5 minutes on each side until golden brown and cooked. Rest the fish on a kitchen-paper-lined roasting tray. Fry the ginger and chillies in oil for 1 minute; remove. Place the papaya salad on a platter and top with the fish; garnish with ginger, coriander and chillies and pour the remaining sauce over the fish before serving.

KOREAN SPICY SQUID (KOREAN)

Preparation: 5 minutes
Cooking: 20 minutes

serves: 2

80 ml (2½ fl oz/⅓ cup) Sweet & Spicy Sauce (see page 28)
1 teaspoon grated fresh ginger
3 tablespoons vegetable oil
½ small onion, chopped
1 carrot, sliced on bias
1 courgette (zucchini), halved and sliced
400 g (14 oz) squid, sliced into rings
2 spring onions (scallions), sliced into 4 cm (1½ inch) pieces
1 tablespoon toasted sesame oil

recipe

Mix the sauce with the ginger. Heat the oil in a wok, add the vegetables, except the spring onions, and stir-fry for 5–8 minutes until tender. Set aside. Add the squid to the wok and cook for 3 minutes until semi-opaque. Add the spring onions and then the ginger sauce and stir for 5 minutes until combined and the squid is cooked. Add the vegetables and stir together. Remove from the heat, drizzle with the sesame oil and combine. Divide between 2 bowls and season, if needed.

CRÊPE WITH PRAWNS (VIETNAMESE)

Preparation: 10 minutes
Cooking: 5–10 minutes

serves: 2

140 g (5 oz/scant 1 cup) rice flour
½ teaspoon ground turmeric
½ teaspoon salt
175 ml (6 fl oz/⅔ cup) coconut milk
2 spring onions (scallions), sliced into 3 cm (1¼ in) pieces
3 tablespoons vegetable oil
250 g (9 oz) raw prawns, peeled, deveined and halved lengthways
80 g (3 oz) mung beansprouts
40 g (1½ oz) onion, thinly sliced
4 pieces of red leaf lettuce, shredded
60 ml (2 fl oz/¼ cup) Nuoc Cham Base sauce (see page 22), for dipping

recipe

Whisk the flour, turmeric, salt, 175 ml (6 fl oz/⅔ cup) of water, coconut milk and spring onions together. Heat 1 tablespoon of oil in a wok and cook the prawns for 3–5 minutes until opaque and pink. Season and set aside. Heat 1 tablespoon of oil in the wok over medium heat. Pour in 100 ml (3½ fl oz) of batter and swirl gently, letting the batter coat the base and sides of the wok. Cook for 1 minute until the batter looks dry. Place two prawn pieces, the sprouts and onions on half of the crêpe and fold over; transfer to a plate. Repeat. Serve with the shredded lettuce and sauce.

WHOLE STEAMED FISH (CHINESE)

Preparation: 15 minutes
Cooking: 15 minutes

serves: 2

2 tablespoons soy sauce
1 tablespoon rice vinegar
1 red bird's-eye chilli, julienned
1 whole fish, such as snapper (about 450–500 g/1 lb–1 lb 2 oz), cleaned
40 g (1½ oz) piece of fresh ginger, peeled and julienned
130 ml (4½ fl oz/½ cup) Sichuan Oil (see page 30)
2 spring onions (scallions), white and light green parts thinly sliced

recipe

Combine the soy sauce, vinegar and chilli. Season the fish; stuff half of the ginger in the fish cavity and the other half on top. Fill the wok with 120 ml (4 fl oz/½ cup) of water. Place the fish on a plate in a steamer in the wok. Heat the wok over medium-high heat and bring to the boil; covered. Steam for 10 minutes, or until cooked through. Place the fish on a serving dish. Heat the oil in the wok until piping hot. Place the spring onions on top of the fish; drizzle with the hot oil and soy sauce mixture.

TURMERIC-DILL FISH (VIETNAMESE)

Preparation: 10 minutes + Refrigeration: 2 hours
Cooking: 5 to 8 minutes

176

serves: 2

2 pieces of white fish, such as cod, about 175 g (6 oz) each
salt and freshly ground black pepper
2 tablespoons fish sauce
½ teaspoon ground turmeric
2 garlic cloves, finely chopped
3 cm (1¼ in) knob of fresh ginger, peeled and finely chopped
20 g (¾ oz) dill, plus extra to garnish
2 tablespoons grapeseed oil
200 g (7 oz) cooked vermicelli noodles (85 g/3 oz uncooked)
10 g (½ oz) mixed herbs, such as mint leaves, Thai basil leaves and sliced spring onions (scallions)
4 tablespoons Nuoc Cham Base Sauce (see page 22), for dipping

recipe

Season the fish. Combine the fish sauce, turmeric, garlic, ginger and half of the dill. Add the fish and refrigerate for 2 hours. Remove the excess marinade from the fish and pat dry. Heat the wok over high heat, add the oil and the fish and cook for 4–5 minutes on each side until cooked. Add the remaining dill and sauté for 2–3 minutes. Divide the noodles between 2 bowls, top with the fish and garnish with herbs. Serve with the sauce.

THAI-STYLE SALMON SALAD (THAI)

Preparation: 25 minutes
Cooking: 5 minutes

serves: 2

2 salmon fillets (about 350 g/12 oz), skinned and sliced into 1.5 cm (⅝ in) pieces
2 tablespoons grapeseed oil
2 Granny Smith apples, julienned
65 g (2¼ oz) red (bell) pepper, julienned
¼ small red onion, thinly sliced
20 g (¾ oz) coriander (cilantro), roughly chopped
8 g (¼ oz) Thai basil, roughly chopped
1 tablespoon roasted peanuts, crushed, plus extra to garnish
60 ml (2 fl oz/¼ cup) Nuoc Cham Base sauce (see page 22), for dipping

recipe

Season the salmon. Heat the oil in a wok until just about smoking, add the salmon and sear and crisp for 2–3 minutes on each side until opaque and pink. Meanwhile, combine the remaining ingredients, except the peanuts nuoc cham, and toss together. Divide the slaw between 2 bowls, add the salmon, broken into pieces, and garnish with peanuts. Serve with the sauce.

CALAMARI WITH CHILLI SAUCE (THAI)

Preparation: 10 minutes
Cooking: 15–20 minutes

180

serves: 2

365 g (13 oz) squid, tubes sliced and tentacles whole
100 g (3½ oz/generous ½ cup) potato flour
salt and freshly ground black pepper
175 ml (6 fl oz/⅔ cup) vegetable oil
2 cucumbers, thinly sliced
½ red onion, thinly sliced
15 g (½ oz) mint, chopped
15 g (½ oz) coriander (cilantro), chopped
2 tablespoons Nuoc Cham Base Sauce (see page 22)
60 ml (2 fl oz/¼ cup) sweet chilli sauce, for dipping

recipe

Toss the squid in potato flour and salt and pepper until well coated. Place on a baking tray in one layer. Heat the oil in a wok over medium-high heat until it reaches 180°C (350°F). Add the squid in four batches and fry for 3–5 minutes. Drain on a kitchen-paper-lined roasting tray. Combine the remaining ingredients, except the sweet chilli sauce, and toss together. Serve the calamari with the cucumber salad and sweet chilli sauce for dipping.

LEMONGRASS SCALLOPS (VIETNAMESE)

Preparation: 10 minutes
Cooking: 10 minutes

182

serves: 2

2 tablespoons vegetable oil
350 g (12 oz) scallops
25 g (1 oz) finely chopped lemongrass
3 garlic cloves, finely chopped
1 shallot, sliced
1 red chilli, sliced
2 teaspoons Stir-fry Sauce (see page 18)
1 tablespoon fish sauce
90 g (3¼ oz) mixed salad leaves
lime wedges, to garnish

recipe

Heat 1 tablespoon of oil in a wok, add the scallops and sear for 3–5 minutes on each side until golden brown. Set aside. Add the remaining oil and lemongrass, garlic, shallot and chilli and stir-fry for 1 minute until fragrant. Return the scallops to the wok with the remaining ingredients, except the salad and limes, and stir-fry for 2–3 minutes. Divide the salad leaves between 2 bowls and top with the scallops and lime.

HONEY WALNUT PRAWNS (CHINESE)

Preparation: 15 minutes
Cooking: 10 minutes

184

serves: 2

3 tablespoons mayonnaise
1 tablespoon honey
1 tablespoon sweetened condensed milk
1 teaspoon lemon juice
salt and freshly ground black pepper
330 g (11½ oz) raw prawns, peeled and deveined, with tails on
1 egg yolk, beaten
80 g (3 oz/generous ½ cup) tempura flour
175 ml (6 fl oz/⅔ cup) safflower oil
60 g (2 oz/½ cup) walnut halves

recipe

Whisk together the mayonnaise, honey, condensed milk and lemon juice. Season the prawns and dip into the beaten egg, then the flour; set aside. Heat the oil in a wok over a high heat until it reaches 180°C (350°F). Fry the prawns for 2–3 minutes until golden brown. Drain on a kitchen-paper-lined baking tray in one layer. Add the prawns to the mayo honey mixture and mix to combine. Divide between 2 bowls and top with walnuts.

SAFFRON MUSSELS (THAI)

Preparation: 10 minutes
Cooking: 15 minutes

serves: 2

1 tablespoon coconut oil
2 shallots, sliced
120 ml (4 fl oz/½ cup) Coconut Base Sauce (see page 26)
2 lemongrass stalks, trimmed and thinly chopped
large pinch of saffron threads
1 red chilli, sliced
450 g (1 lb) live mussels, cleaned and de-bearded
2 spring onions (scallions), sliced on bias, to garnish
30 g (1 oz) coriander (cilantro), to garnish

recipe

Heat the oil in a wok over medium-high heat, add the shallots and cook for 2–3 minutes until translucent. Add 2½ tablespoons of water and the remaining ingredients, except the mussels, spring onions and coriander, and bring to the boil. Add the mussels, cover and simmer until the mussels open, about 2-3 minutes. Uncover and stir for 5 minutes until combined and all the mussels are open. Divide the broth and mussels into 2 bowls and top with spring onions and coriander.

TAMARIND WHITE FISH (THAI)

Preparation: 10 minutes
Cooking: 15 minutes

serves: 2

2 teaspoons tamarind pulp
2 shallots, finely sliced
2 tablespoons grated fresh ginger
15 g (½ oz) coriander (cilantro) with stems, roughly chopped, plus extra to garnish
2 teaspoons sugar
1 tablespoon fish sauce
2 firm white fish fillets, such as cod
1 tablespoon Pickled Bird's-eye Chillies (see page 34) (optional)

recipe

Heat the tamarind, 60 ml (2 fl oz/¼ cup) of water, shallots, ginger, coriander, sugar and fish sauce in a wok over medium-high heat and stir until the tamarind and sugar are dissolved. Add the fish to the sauce, cover and cook for 10 minutes, or until cooked through. Divide between 2 plates and top with extra coriander. Serve with pickled chillies, if desired.

INDEX

WITHDRAWN

ACKNOWLEDGEMENTS

Thanks to Catie Ziller for another opportunity to create a book of my favourite Asian dishes. As always, a special appreciative note to Kathy Steer for her editorial notes and thanks to Michelle for making this book look good and for her great drawings.

This book wouldn't have happened without the help of Jessica Darakjian and Kaitlyn Kisser, always making sure the shoot days went smoothly. And again, my endless gratitude to Julia Stotz for her sense of humour and for her photography making the food look beautiful. Finally, thanks to my two best friends, my husband, Joel Speasmaker and Lisa Butterworth. Without their support, I wouldn't know how to get through a hard day or any day.

First published by © Hachette Livre (Marabout) 2016
The English language edition published in 2018 by Hardie Grant Books, an imprint of Hardie Grant Publishing

Hardie Grant Books (London)
5th & 6th Floors
52–54 Southwark Street
London SE1 1UN

Hardie Grant Books (Melbourne)
Building 1, 658 Church Street
Richmond, Victoria 3121

hardiegrantbooks.com

Text © Caroline Hwang 2018
Photography © Julia Stotz 2018

British Library Cataloguing-in-Publication Data. A catalogue record for this book is available from the British Library.

ISBN 978-1-78488-154-2

Publisher: Catie Ziller
Photography: Julia Stotz
Design: Michelle Tilly
Editor: Kathy Steer

For the English edition:

Publisher: Kate Pollard
Commissioning Editor: Kajal Mistry
Desk Editor: Molly Ahuja
Publishing Assistant: Eila Purvis
Editor: Kay Halsey

Colour Reproduction by p2d
Printed and bound in China by 1010